Contents

Editor
Greg Payne

Design Editor
Liz Wright

Origination
Sally Robinson

Published by
Greenlight Publishing
The Publishing House, 119 Newland Street,
Witham, Essex CM8 1WF
Tel: 01376 521900   Fax: 01376 521901
email: info@greenlightpublishing.co.uk
www.greenlightpublishing.co.uk

Printed
in Great Britain

ISBN 1 897738 153
© 2003 Greenlight Publishing

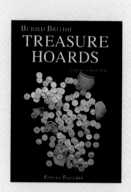
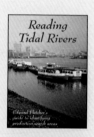

Introduction

How many British detectorists have found pre-Victorian coins or artefacts on coastal sites around our shores? There have certainly been one or two spectacular discoveries, including gold nobles, moneyboxes stuffed with hammered silver pennies, Iron Age jewellery, Viking swords, and even Roman bronze statues. Those headline grabbers stick in our memories; but it's my considered opinion that the overwhelming majority of amateur treasure hunters who have gone down to the seaside anticipating historical finds have returned home very disappointed, even when their pockets bulged with modern money and jewellery. Enthusiasm for beach work has taken such a blow from these experiences that it's probable that very many readers of this book have made a detecting trip to the coast only once during their years of involvement in the hobby. Once was more than enough.

Why have these disappointments occurred time and time again? Surely the fundamental law of losses states that coins and artefacts will be found in places where people have congregated in the past? After all, people have lived and worked on coastal land for thousands of years. Yet the infallible law seems to fail us when we rely on its infallibility down by the seaside. Something is, indeed, amiss. Nevertheless, my faith in the old law remains steadfast. I'm convinced that almost all past failures can be accounted for by one or more of the factors listed below.

Wrong Type Of Metal Detector Used

Most detectorists interested in medieval and ancient coins and relics (I include myself here) have bought and learned to use detectors that work extremely well on the sort of plough soil found in arable fields flanking medieval and ancient habitation sites. A browse through the past 20 years' issues of **Treasure Hunting** magazine reveals many of our inland successes. Long may they continue. But the machines that brought forth such exciting discoveries on inland sites do not perform well on wet salt sand, the very spots where their owners probably attempted to use them on the coast.

Wrong Time Of Year

If your interest in history draws you to pre-Victorian sites you will obviously want to work them in autumn and winter when fields are bare or still accessible with the landowner's approval. You would not dream of wasting a precious autumn or winter weekend on a trip to the seaside. It seems logical to leave such sites for summer months when arable fields are knee-deep in crops. Unfortunately, the middle of summer happens to be just about the worst time for working beaches. Sand will be deep; storms highly unlikely; the only potential discoveries within range in the soft, dry sand at the top of the beach, or the wet stuff down by the tide line, will be recent losses. Who can blame a detectorist accustomed to returning from a plough soil site with two or three hammered and an ornate brooch or strap end for feeling that he/she has failed on the foreshore when there's nothing but spendable loose change in the finds bag?

Wrong Location

Few detectorists feel inclined to invest valuable time in investigating the histories of sites they expect to visit no more than once a year, and even less inclined when those types of sites seem always associated with modern losses. If you regard coastal trips as no more than a means of keeping your hand in, or of simply not allowing your detector-swinging arm to stiffen up, it's hardly surprising that very little serious investigation of the site's potential gets done beforehand. Any holiday resort within reasonable driving distance will suffice. If you can recall childhood excursions to the place; if your grandma told you that she pitched her deck-chair near the bandstand; if the parking meters can be fed with beach-found money; or if the parking spaces are not too far from the beach, why bother with research?

I hope that many readers of this book have made all three of those mistakes. I certainly did, and not only as a beginner. Decades flew by before I realised the wastefulness of my prejudice against coastal locations. Now I'm bubbling with positive enthusiasm for all things maritime, although I still can't bring myself to enjoy searches for modern money on holiday beaches. I've found other things to do on the shoreline. I can now look at an Explorer coastal map and feel excited by its potential as a research document. And I know that if I read the clues correctly I can now pinpoint spots along almost any coastal region that will offer fair or better prospects for prehistoric artefacts such as flint arrow heads and for much older fossil remains, for Celtic metalwork, for Romano-British losses, for Anglo-Saxon relics, for Norman, Tudor, Stuart, Georgian coins, and for Victorian and Edwardian sovereigns and half-sovereigns. Yes, it is true that I've had to go to the expense of obtaining an additional detector that performs well on wet salt sand, but the good news is that some of the coastal sites I now work lie above the beach and often in places that prove ideal for my regular plough soil detector. I even have the possibility of eyes-only finds now that I've learned to spot and interpret the clues. Anyone who reads what follows and heeds the advice will soon match my successes.

Take the first and most important step now: jettison any notions that beach work means no more than detecting on holiday resort seafronts in summer. Expand your definition of beaches to include the entire coastline, whatever its make-up, running alongside coastal industrial sites and farmland. Expand it inland, too. Reading a beach often means reading clues that will guide you to adjacent dry land rather than onto the beach and down to the water. If what I'm about to reveal convinces you that the coast offers serious site potential you will now be prepared to invest some of your autumn and winter searching time on seaside trips. With your latest detector and a combination of stormy weather and the right tidal conditions, those popular seaside resorts will also increase enormously in productivity. The awesome power of crashing waves should add a bounty of historical discoveries to your finds bag.

Please read this book from cover to cover before trying your luck at site finding. Absorbing its contents entirely will go a long way towards altering your views on beaches. Let me also add (it's more than sales pitch) that readers who now possess all three books in my Greenlight trilogy will be in a very favourable position when it comes to reading beaches. In view of what I've just said about expanding the definition of beaches, some of the contents of **Reading Land** will apply here. Similarly, the point at which a tidal river estuary becomes a coastal foreshore may have an obscure legal definition; but a lot of the foreshore features discussed in **Reading Rivers** also occur beyond the river mouth.

1. Eyes Only

Not long ago I read an archaeological report about discoveries made when a group of local enthusiasts decided to map ancient and historical features spotted during an eyes-only survey of the English and Welsh foreshores along the Bristol Channel. Among many unexpected encounters was an area where a strong tidal current had stripped loose sand from several hundred square yards of beach to leave an ancient peat bed exposed between high and low water. Examining the black surface, the archaeologists noticed numerous flint fragments embedded in the peat. Some were quite obviously man-made artefacts: barbed arrow and spear heads that had first felt the touch of a human hand more than 10,000 years ago when Neolithic hunters tracked and killed game in a marshland landscape of reeds and grasses. The vegetation died and rotted to form peat beds that were engulfed by the sea many centuries later.

In a book about scuba diving in Britain's shallow coastal waters I read with a little amusement that some diving clubs around the Solent have "adopted" several wooden hulks spotted on local foreshores. The divers practice their underwater archaeology techniques with the aid of what looks like a children's climbing frame. Placed in position on the foreshore, and directly over one of the hulks, the frame allows trainees to stay dry while obtaining a swimmer's eye view of what an undiscovered wreck lying a few hundred yards off-shore might look like. The foreshore hulks have, on investigation, almost all proved to be timber-built Georgian and Victorian fishing vessels.

A newspaper headline caught my eye not long ago: "Boy Spots Dinosaur Footprints On Beach". I read the piece and learned that the lad had gone to the south coast with a school party. They were looking for fossils, and they were searching a stretch of coastline on which thousands of people have searched in the past. Nevertheless, the sharp-eyed kid noticed the ancient tracks, about 65 million years after the dinosaur walked there.

On another occasion I skimmed the pages of a privately published booklet on the history of a Kentish parish. The writer's interest in the subject had begun during a walk along the lonely and rather featureless coastline of his community. At one spot the sea had eroded the edges of a flanking field where sheep and cattle grazed, indifferent to the fact that the sea also grazes, and that it is slowly eating its way inland. A pile of newly fallen soil lay at the top of the beach; on closer inspection it revealed fragments of Roman and Anglo-Saxon pottery, vital clues to a nearby ancient habitation site.

Clearly all four of the above incidents show that metal detecting is not the only way to make discoveries on the coast. Eyes-only works exceptionally well on foreshores that receive a thorough scouring by tides and currents twice in 24 hours. But there's a much more important lesson to be learned here: my own eyes had to work to discover these sites. Reading will produce similar results for you, but you must apply yourself to the task diligently. It's not enough to scan the meagre history shelves at a local branch library conveniently close to your home. Reading for research purposes calls for greater effort.

Begin by choosing a coastal region on which you can concentrate your attention. I recommend the nearest coastal county, especially if the county town lies within easy reach. Anyone lucky enough to live close to a wide estuary with two or more county borders on its flanks has even better prospects. But don't take on too much. Invest in your own **OS Explorer** maps, even if you have to buy two or three to cover the full length of your region. With access to a good photocopier you can make enlargements of the coastal sections (200% is ideal) and then re-copy the copies so that you can keep one set at home and take another set with you on further stages of your eyes-only research campaign.

The local history section of the county library should be your next destination. If the shelves appear well-stocked, don't grumble. Masses of useful information awaits your eyes. Develop a skim reading technique, but don't confuse skimming with skimping. Train your eyes to spot words such as foreshore, erosion, wreck, archaeology, fishing, fossils and other keys. I always open any history book at the back and spend a few minutes reading the index. A well-indexed book is the hallmark of a good historian, although I have to admit that many a gem of crucial information has come from obscure works with no index to ease the task of having to skim every page to locate those gems.

Mark on your photocopied maps the grid references of any interesting spots you identify with accuracy from the author's words. If she/he provides maps and diagrams, transfer the information to your own maps when it mentions any feature on or near the coastline. Anything and everything to do with the foreshore merits a pencilled entry. Write your notes on the seaward side of the map and at 90 degrees to the coastline, with a pencilled line to the relevant spot on the beach. Over time your photocopied map will become littered with scribbled notes, which you will have to tidy up by transferring the information more succinctly to a fresh photocopy. I use T-line shorthand when making my notes; you might devise a system of symbols, abbreviations, or even coloured pencils. Some of the information you record may never prove useful; other snippets might seem irrelevant until another word, sentence or paragraph catches your skimming eye months or even years, later. Together they may suddenly open your eyes to something of crucial importance that leads to exciting finds. A glaringly obvious example will record the finding of a single high-value coin on an isolated stretch of beach. A decade later, following a stormy night, another coin, similar in value and age, turns up on the same spot. Less obvious might be the recording of ancient pottery fragments on a beach, followed decades later by news that farm fields flanking that spot have been sold to a developer with plans for a housing estate.

Here's a selection of some of the pencilled notes I've made on coastal maps in the past as a direct result of reading local history books:-

"shipwreck 1844.....caves.....derelict lime kiln..... vanished DMV.....Roman coins found 1950.....ferry.....fossil beds.....ancient causeway.....former fishing port.....possible Viking landings here.....cliff steps.....gap in ancient seawall.....county boundary marker.....wooden hulk on beach.....severe flooding 17th century.....fish curing sheds 19th century.....Armada beacon on cliff top.....military encampment 18th century".

Even if your county library yields a crop of potential sites as exciting as those listed above, you have examined no more than the tip of a veritable iceberg-sized research source available to you via a single library membership card. The Inter-Library Loans Service operates to ensure that almost any library book in every public library in the land can be borrowed by any reader who asks to read it. Study the bibliographies and "sources of further information" provided by the authors whose books you come across. Note title, author, publisher and year of publication for any book you would like to read. Obtain the necessary application form from the enquiries desk and you will probably have the book in your hands in a week or two, provided there's a copy available for public library borrowing.

Readers whose interest in coastal locations extends beyond public library resources can gain access to academic libraries and undertake further research. I have used academic libraries in three ways. Firstly, by enrolling on a university course and obtaining a undergraduate's library card. I read for my degree in the days when educational grants were still available. Times have changed. A less expensive way into university libraries is to apply for an external reader's ticket. Mine, from universities in London, have cost around £50 per year per library, a price worth paying when dozens of visits to the library's book stacks seem likely.

On another occasion I needed access to a scholarly book to check facts for a single article. I couldn't justify £50 expenditure, so I approached a student entering the university library and offered him a fiver, a coffee and a sandwich if he would use his ticket to borrow the book in question and let me skim read it in a local coffee bar while he enjoyed the sandwich. He jumped at my offer.

I've never believed that a picture is worth a thousand words; I can paint a memorable picture with 999 words. What I most fervently believe is that Victorian 6in Ordnance Survey maps provide us with vivid illustrations of the land as it looked more than a century ago, and that the images often have more to say than an academic history book or archaeological report. Ireland possesses a wonderful claim to fame: the first country on earth to have its surface mapped accurately at six-inches-to-one-mile. The maps were drawn in the 1820s/30s for the purpose of measuring land holdings so that the British government could enforce its land taxing laws. Modern Irish readers, who are banned from using metal detectors in the Republic thanks to draconian and shortsighted Irish laws, can take comfort from eyes-only searches using information gleaned from those wonderful old maps. British readers can take themselves and their photocopied map segments along to a local county records office where Victorian editions of British OS 6in maps should be available for inspection. Careful comparisons between maps drawn in the 1870s/90s and maps re-surveyed four or five years ago will reveal altered coastlines, diverted streams, differences in the shape of the shore, locations of vanished seawalls, silted harbours, creeks, inlets, offshore islands and much more. Those subjects will receive detailed treatment in the pages that follow. Here, let me provide a single example to show how using your eyes (often with the aid of a magnifying glass) to look closely at old OS maps can put you on the trail of good finds.

We all know that numerous hedgerows have vanished from our landscape during the past 50 years as arable farming became more efficient and landowners turned small fields into huge mono-crop prairies. Things were different in Victorian times when most fields had boundary hedges that enclosed just enough land to keep a ploughman busy for a single day. With that in mind, look closely at Victorian 6in maps of your chosen coastline. If you find places where fields that lie along the coast appear considerably narrower than fields further inland you have strong evidence to suggest that erosion of the coast occurred in Anglo-Saxon or medieval times. Prior to encroachment the fields had boundary fences that made them the same size as other fields in the district. Additional clues such as lanes and footpaths that end abruptly on the seaward side of a field or piles of stones on the adjacent beach will strengthen the case for seeking ancient and medieval losses on that particular shore. You could be on the trail of a lost farmstead, or even a lost hamlet or village.

Surfing seems a most appropriate term for eyes-only searches on the Internet. It can prove rewarding, especially for those who do their research with the aid of Broadband. Hundred of pages devoted to maritime history and archaeology are on offer, but there's a lot of repetition and many pages treat their subjects too lightly, despite the attractive colours and illustrations. If, like me, you prefer the feel of a book to that of a mouse and keyboard, use the Internet to check on opening times at the library and the county records office, and the times of buses and trains to get you there, or to the coast when you set out on an expedition armed with all the knowledge you have gained from eyes-only research. You can also use the net to find and make printed copies of tide tables for any coast and for months ahead in time, enabling you to co-ordinate your trips with spring and neap tides. Combine that information with Internet forecasts of imminent storms and you will give yourself the very best chances of success on the day of your trip.

The research stage of any projected foray to the coast is an excellent time to join forces with fellow enthusiasts and to spread the costs and rewards of reading, photocopying and printing the results of lengthy investigations. Confirm before you throw in your lot with other club members and detecting pals that they share your enthusiasm and that they will diligently apply themselves to whatever research task they undertake. Half-hearted reading and examination of maps and documents wastes everybody's time. So does over-optimistic interpretation of research results. There's no shame in spending many hours investigating what seems initially a possible bonanza site, only to confirm by thorough research that in truth the chances of interesting finds seem highly unlikely. Frank acknowledgement that the group is on the wrong tack not only prevents time wasting - it gives everyone a second chance to get on the right tack with a different site.

2. Clothing, Equipment & Safety

Aware that some of your most productive visits to the coast will take place during autumn and winter, at the height of, or just after, stormy weather, now is the time to check your kit. You probably already have what I call "the detectorist's wardrobe" - anorak, woolly hat, gloves, boots, and other bits and pieces to make life a little more comfortable during days on bare fields. I recently added a pair of kneepads to my ensemble, a benefit to young and old and highly recommended. But for coastal trips you'll need other extras. Waterproof footwear is crucial down at the sea's edge, as are extra layers of clothing. Biting winds will dog your footsteps on most days, so wear thermal vests, thermal gloves and thermal socks. Buy those items from a reputable outdoor equipment retailer; market stall bargains rarely perform well enough to keep out the cold for more than an hour.

I have a pair of chest-length waders in my kit, purchased second-hand from a fisherman, but so far I've used them only for occasional river work. In my opinion the seas around Britain are much too cold for wading to a depth above waist height in the middle of winter. I leave such exploits to scuba divers. But if you plan Continental winter wade-in trips, try to include second-hand waders in your outfit. They weigh a lot, but will prove much less expensive that diver's neoprene, and will suffice for most workable wade-in depths.

As already made clear, a detector capable of top performance on wet salt sand must be added to your gear if you hope to achieve successes on the coast. Let me offer you two fool-proof ways to determine which machine to choose: observe beach enthusiasts at work and buy the same detector as the person who consistently makes the best finds; or read back issues of **Treasure Hunting** to find test reports on beach detectors, as well as first-person articles written by exponents of this branch of the hobby. Be guided by what you read in the editorial pages rather than glossy advertising and sales brochures.

Coastal searching offers plenty of opportunities to experiment with homemade equipment. Floating sieves and sand scoops, many self-designed items, already play important roles in wade-in work. When working on public beaches you can add tools that help with searches around the edges of harbour walls, moorings and other large objects that may have acted as traps for coins and relics. Masses of ironwork often make detecting impossible, so why not dig and sieve the sand or shingle instead? Your minor excavations amount to little more than the sort of sand shifting carried out by children building sand castles on the beach during summer. A small trench at the base of a wall will do as little harm, but please fill in any holes you dig before you leave the beach. A plastic mesh screen held in a simple wooden frame greatly increases the chances of finds at such spots. Use a spade to excavate a trench about a foot deep and two or three yards in length along the base of the wall. Place your screen across part of the trench, then dig deeper and throw the material onto the screen so that it falls back into the excavation. With luck, coins and relics will become trapped in the mesh. Combine that technique with detecting across the plastic mesh and your finds rate should rise dramatically.

The dangers involved in any hobby that requires participants to venture onto bleak foreshores during periods of bad weather cannot be ignored, especially by parents with children eager to enjoy the fun. Let us not forget that youngsters have drowned on holiday beaches recently, and that adults have got into grave difficulties during rescue attempts. Keep kids under close scrutiny at all times if they join you on winter trips to the coast. Everyone who takes part must understand the dangers of rising tides, of dangerous currents no more than knee-deep below the tide line, of quick sands on some beaches, of extremely slippery rocks on many more, of landslips and rock falls onto the beach beneath cliffs, and especially of the dangers of becoming so engrossed in the fun that time slips by unnoticed. Be watchful!

3. Fossils On The Foreshore

Most eastern, south-eastern and southern counties with coastal borders have miles of foreshore where fossils await keen eyes. Finds in recent years have ranged in value from a few pence to several thousand pounds, the latter making news headlines several times following discoveries of complete or near-complete fossilized dinosaurs and other remarkable ancient creatures. Add those financial incentives to the fact that many three and four-year olds can recite and spell correctly names such as diplodocus, plesiosaur, pterodactyl, and brontosaurus at a time when they can't quite tie their own shoelaces, and it's hardly surprising that this branch of amateur treasure hunting attracts more family groups than any other.

If you and your family want to participate, there are one or two general rules to bear in mind, not least the already clearly stated warning that parents must be ever watchful when they take children to coastal locations. Avoid coasts that have strong currents and deep water close inshore; also be aware while searching eroded material at the foot of cliffs, and even when wearing a safety helmet, that you risk injury from falling boulders, especially in winter when previous rainfall might have loosened rocks higher up the cliff face. Despite those restrictions you will still have scores of safe beaches to choose from, and many places where the cliffs are barely 6ft high. Visit them in winter; timing your trips to coincide with low spring tides, and you are sure to make finds.

Don't buy specialist tools. Take one or two items from your DIY kit: a strong penknife, a small hammer, perhaps a couple of chisels. Nature will have done most of the work of loosening fossils from their matrix of harder shale, sand, mud and rocks. You'll use your fingers as much as the few tools I've mentioned. But do remember to take suitable containers to hold your finds. I usually raid the kitchen and borrow small plastic boxes, which I stuff with kitchen paper or strips of damp newspaper. Don't forget the box lids.

Search techniques mirror those used during eyes-only searches for coins and relics on bare soil: keep the sun on your back, scan the foreshore a few yards ahead; seek out symmetrically shaped objects; look for unusual shapes or

Fig.1. Storms combined with high spring tides frequently erode fossil bearing cliffs to add to the easily collected specimens already on the foreshore.

patterns on large rocks; let brighter or different colours catch your eye; pick up anything that attracts your attention. As with fields, the foreshore surface benefits from heavy rainfall, especially if the rain comes down on sand and shingle not long after a very high tide has swept up the beach and washed over any scree beneath cliffs. Fossils in larger boulders will also show much more clearly when the rock is wet with rain.

Low cliffs behind the beach should be searched for bands of softer sand or clay sandwiched between harder rocks. Rake these softer beds and you might find fossils that would otherwise take many years to reach the beach via the natural processes of erosion.

Fig2. Sharks' teeth up to 50 million years old picked up during a stroll on a Kentish beach.

Adult searchers unencumbered by youngsters will make better finds if they climb on rather higher cliff faces noted as fossil collecting sites. Restrict your efforts to dry days; it can be extremely dangerous to climb even a few feet up wet cliffs; however, mild the gradient. Steer well clear of vertical cliffs on rainy days.

What can you expect to find? Well, I can't guarantee a dinosaur, although I would not be surprised to hear about at least one reader discovering such a creature within a year of this book's publication. Meanwhile make interesting collections of the commoner items: ammonites, sharks' teeth, ancient crabs, lobsters, shells, entire fish skeletons and numerous fish bones and scales, fossilized shells galore, ancient plants, sponges, corrals, fossilized wood, insects, turtles, the fragmentary remains of prehistoric crocodiles, snakes, ichthyosaurs, plesiosaurs, even dinosaur's footprints. They have all come to light around our shores in substantial numbers. No, there's no single beach where you'll find the lot. But if you make regular trips to even a quarter of the places listed below, and if you search diligently for several hours during each trip you should own a respectable collection of fossils within 12 months.

Fig.3. Ammonite fossils.

Yorkshire

Almost any accessible beach between Redcar and the mouth of the Humber has fossils awaiting collection. Dedicated enthusiasts concentrate on hot spots such as Ravenscar, Whitby, Sandsend, Scarborough, Reighton Gap, Filey, Robin Hood's Bay, Cayton Bay, Speeton, Runswick Bay, Bempton and Danes Dyke.

East Anglia

Although not so richly endowed with fossils as Yorkshire, there are one or two interesting locations including South Ferriby, Overstrand and Covehithe where you should make good finds.

Essex

We are back on rich hunting grounds on these coasts. Try your luck at Walton-on-Naze, Wrabness, Harwich and Maylandsea.

Kent

Folkestone offers good prospects.

Sussex

You are entering Jurassic country. Numerous dinosaur bones have come to light on the beaches between Hastings and Fairlight. Hastings and Eastbourne have rich foreshores holding many other interesting fossils.

Hampshire

There are said to be more than 500 different types of fossilized shells to find on the beaches of this county. Large sharks' teeth also frequently come to light. Hot spots include Barton-on-Sea and Milford-on-Sea.

Isle Of Wight

A paradise for fossil hunters and the region that has produced the most spectacular dinosaur remains. Benbridge, Rocken End, Whale Chine, Whitecliff Bay, Yaverland and Blackgang Chine should all be visited during trips to the island. There are numerous fossils worth discovering even if you fail to spot a dinosaur.

Dorset

This county is famous in fossil collecting lore as the place where it all started. Lyme Regis has been the scene of numerous spectacular discoveries of the bones of ancient creatures, but the county has even more to offer. As well as a trip to Lyme Regis, try your luck at Burton Bradstock, Charmouth, Durlston Bay and Portland.

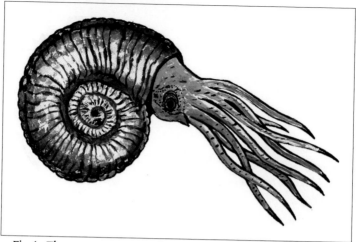

Fig.4. The strange creature that occupied the ammonite shell 65 million years ago.

Devon

Devon has almost as many fossil-rich beaches as Yorkshire. You can choose from Pinhay Bay, Budleigh Salterton, Beer Head, Croyde, Woolacombe, Exmouth, Lynmouth, Fremington and Seaton to be sure of finds.

Somerset

Watchet, Quantoxhead, Kilve, Blue Anchor, Minehead, St Andries Bay and Donfield Bay are all worth exploring. As well as ancient fish, some of these beaches are noted for their ammonite fossils.

Avon

A small coastal strip, but the foreshores around Aust hold fascinating fossils including ichthyosaur and plesiosaur bones.

Dyfed

A trip to Wales is worth the effort if you can come home with a trilobite. Try your luck on the shores around Abereiddy.

4. Flint Artefacts

An archaeological report concerning a 1970s excavation on a Roman villa in what we now call Leicestershire can surely have little to tell us about coastal foreshores? The county is landlocked and about as far from the sea as it's possible to get in island Britain. But tucked away on page 43 of the report there's a list of finds from the archaeologists' trenches: coins, fibulae, buckles, strap ends, potsherds...and several hundred oyster shells, mussel shells, cockle shells and fish bone fragments. This villa was quite small and not richly endowed with statues and mosaic pavements. Had it been the country estate of a high-ranking Roman official, the report might also have mentioned jars of preserved fish, even anchovy paste imported from Hispania. Such finds often turn up. What puzzles me is that the excavators seem to do little more than record what they discover; discussion about the implications scarcely merits a sentence or two. Let me do better and give the matter an entire paragraph.

If minor Roman villas in rural Britannia had seafood on their weekly menus we can infer a substantial coastal fishing industry to keep demand and supply in balance. Fresh oysters remain in that condition for five days at most unless refrigerated; the rotting time for fish is much shorter unless smoked quite soon after landing. If Romano-British villas, villages, towns and forts were to enjoy the fruits of the sea once or twice a week, fishermen must have worked at their trade with equal regularity. Other people must have invested time and money in buying catches wholesale, and in setting up supply routes along rivers, as well as inland retail markets where country folk could do their shopping. So the coast's abundance as a source of food was widely exploited in Roman times. Something similar, if on a smaller scale, had gone on over many generations before the legions arrived.

Three thousand years earlier some of Britain's first human communities also exploited the coasts, at first as easy routes for travellers on foot, but very soon as a rich and varied source of food. Bear in mind that sea levels have in general risen over several thousand years. Today's inter-tidal zone was, in those days, low-lying ground where reeds,

23

Fig.5. Deadly weapons and ancient works of art. Ideal conditions for seeking flint arrowheads include black peat on the foreshore, gentle sunshine on the searcher's back, and a shower of rain recently fallen. When all three occur together flint artefacts stand out clearly as the sun's rays strike their multi-faceted surfaces.

grasses, shrubs, even belts of trees, grew abundantly - a paradise for deer, boar, goats, hares and birds, with oysters, mussels, cockles, seaweeds, crabs, fish and eels available in the flanking sea. When nature works to our benefit and washes away coverings of sand and shingle to leave dark peat or sticky clay exposed for a few days we can often catch glimpses of life in those distant times. They take the form of flint artefacts, usually barbed arrowheads and fishhooks with larger flint tools occasionally turning up. Each represents a miss by the hunter or fisherman who shot the arrow or hurled the spear; the barb was either lost in a tangle of reeds and grass, or it vanished beneath the waves.

Under favourable conditions flint is easy to spot as an eyes-only find. Its colour can vary from milky white to dark grey, but it always reflects light. Against a background of black peat or grey/brown tidal mud and clay it will leap to your eye if you keep the sun on your back while walking the foreshore as the tide falls. Improve your chances of discovering artefacts by searching where people have found them in the past. In other words, do your reading research long before you set out on a quest for flint artefacts.

When researching or marking-up maps, always record past finds of worked flints discovered on cliff tops. Several thousand years ago the same sea cliffs might have taken the

Fig.6. A band of peaty clay exposed when strong currents swept away a covering of sand.

form of an escarpment overlooking an area of reeds and grasses and providing a panoramic view of the sea. Ancient hunters would have used the vantage point to watch for flocks of birds or herds of deer moving into their killing grounds. Fishermen would have scanned the sea and spotted shoals of migratory fish moving into shallow feeding grounds in the bay below. The men probably made some of their weapon points during those spells of waiting and watching.

If modern ploughing has taken place on fields close to cliffs always try to gain permission for eyes-only searches of the soil during winter. At one ploughed cliff-top site in Wales more than 40,000 worked flint objects, as well as many shale beads, were discovered largely by fieldwalkers. Identical finds came from the foot of the cliff when the local beach lost much of its sand during stormy weather. Shale (occasionally jet) beads and buttons turn up on many sites where flint artefacts occur. They may prove more difficult to spot due to their black or dark grey colour, especially at places were peat or very dark soil is exposed. Train your eye to spot symmetric shapes and you'll soon add specimens to your finds bag.

5. Fish Traps

Unless you go abroad, perhaps to Asia or Africa, you may never see a coastal fish trap in operation, although one or two survive in Britain on important salmon and/or eel fishing rivers. Two hundred years ago every accessible foreshore around our coastline had traps of various shapes, designs and materials, worked by local fishing families, who usually combined trapping with shared ownership of an inshore fishing vessel. When weather and tides made boat fishing too dangerous the traps could be relied on to put food on family tables, hopefully with surplus fish for sale inland.

Two basic types can be distinguished, although no two were exactly alike, and both types relied for success on the fact that tides move along the foreshore as well as up and down between high and low marks. The first caught and killed fish carried along the beach by a rising tide and strong currents and into a barrier of stakes, nets or wattle fences running across the foreshore. The fish, often migratory shoals, were trapped by their gills and drowned. The second caught fish on a falling tide with a series of stone and/or timber walls that enticed shoals to swim into cul-de-sacs and become trapped in holding ponds higher up the foreshore.

The remains of extremely large examples of both types have come to light in recent years. In Essex an exceptionally low tide in 1997 revealed a series of V-shaped timber posts supporting numerous fragments of wattle hurdles. Each arm of the enormous structure measured more than 1,000yd and each was made up of approximately 13,000 posts. Radiocarbon tests confirmed a Saxon date for this huge trap's construction.

In Wales a single wall of an early medieval "cored" (= fish weir) is estimated to have required 2,000 tons of rocks and boulders. Six multi-walled weirs of similar size have been identified in the same area. They continued in use for hundreds of years. One was so profitable in the 14th century that frequent power struggles broke out between barons and monks over how to carve up the earnings. In the 1700s another was "catching forty pounds worth of mackerel during a single tide"; a third trapped "thirty-five thousand

Fig.7. A 20th century fish trap on a site that has witnessed more than 1,000 years of continuous use. This type catches shoals of fish migrating up the coast on a rising tide. Intimate knowledge of the effects of winds and barometric pressure on the height to which each tide will rise and fall is essential if the fishermen are to catch the maximum number of fish.

herring" in 1850. Many other large-scale traps must lie unseen just below present-day low tide lines. We have to bear in mind that on most coasts sea levels have risen since the traps were constructed. An exceptionally low tide might bring them into view, although many of the losses associated with traps would have occurred further up the foreshore, or on land directly behind the foreshore, where money usually changed hands.

Because local geography and geology played such an important part in determining where a fish trap would work best, the same locations were used and reused by succeeding generations. Nowhere was this more clearly demonstrated than at a fish trap site in Denmark where archaeologists unearthed pieces of ancient timber and basketwork from exposed foreshore peat. Analysis confirmed that some of the timbers dated from the 18th century; other pieces had been hammered into the tidal clay by Vikings; even more fragments produced radiocarbon dates that showed they had been used in fish traps put into place by Neolithic fishing folk more that 5,000 years ago.

How might you set about pinpointing the location of a

vanished fish trap where medieval (perhaps earlier) coins and artefacts await discovery nearby? Begin with any available written sources. Fish traps and weirs often receive mention in local history books, especially if they became the subject of legal disputes over ownership or fishing rights. Try local 6in OS maps as a second line of enquiry. Stone walling and lines of timber posts on a coastal foreshore would certainly have merited recording if visible at the time the map was drawn. Pay particular attention to road and footpath patterns near any location where you suspect a fish trap might once have operated. Paths and minor roads converging on a gap in a seawall, or on a sandy stretch of beach on an otherwise rocky coast, certainly merit attention from detectorists.

When severe storms redistribute the loose material on your local foreshore keep your eyes open for the remains of timber posts or tumbled walls of large boulders. Depressions on an otherwise flat coastline might have been constructed by earlier fishermen as holding pools where catches were kept alive as long as possible. Search the foreshore, tides permitting, around any pinpointed site. Look for flat patches of sand or shingle that might have served as temporary market areas. If local footpaths appear to converge on a particular place, flat or otherwise, they indicate that something quite important went on there in the past. Don't forget the land immediately behind the beach. If it's ploughed and accessible you should soon make finds associated with the local trap-fishing business.

I want to stress at this point the crucial importance of taking what I call a holistic view, not only of fish-traps, but also of foreshore sites of all types, and especially of sites discussed on later pages. Once you have confirmed a location, or if you have tried your luck at the spot and made one or two interesting discoveries, think about how the location fits in with neighbouring geography and geology. Six-inch maps provide the bird's eye view needed. Study contours, river and stream courses, footpaths and bridleways, parish boundaries and the relationship of the site to any nearby settlement or former settlement. Where might money or barter goods connected with beach activities have changed hands? Where might people have congregated before or after doing whatever went on down at the water's edge? Reading beaches is always about reading adjacent land.

6. Ports

In modern usage a port is a place where ships can load and unload while afloat and tied to a dock or harbour wall. Most southerners probably think of cross-Channel ferry ports such as Dover, Harwich and Felixstowe whenever the word comes up in conversation. Readers from the north or west might bring to mind the once bustling fishing ports of Frazerborough and Grimsby, or deep-water terminals such as Milford Haven. But I want to use the word with a much earlier meaning: a place where a shallow-draught and often flat-bottomed vessel could safely beach to off-load or take aboard cargo and passengers.

Fifteen hundred years ago the coasts all around Britain had ports in that sense in every estuary and creek mouth, in every cove with a gently sloping beach, on every flat stretch of shingle or stones. These were all places where coastal sailing ships of 10 to 20 tons "burthen" or "deadweight" (=carrying capacity) could sail up the foreshore at mid-tide and run aground to sit squarely on the bottom as the tide receded. By the 1400s many vessels were equipped with a simple crane used to lift cargoes and swing them over the side onto horse-drawn carts or into packhorse panniers. The carts and packhorse teams went out across the foreshore to the vessel. That's where money and goods changed hands. Any passengers simply scrambled aboard or disembarked straight onto the beach with the aid of a short ladder. By the 1600s ships up to 80ft long and able to carry 40 tons of cargo were trading all around our coasts; by early Victorian times they were 100ft long and carrying 50 tons. Yet almost all of them relied on the ancient practice of beaching at mid-tide to ply their trades.

Let me pause for a moment and ask your obvious question: why did Britain need so many ports during centuries when the economy and the population were considerably smaller than we have today? I'll answer it by reminding you that Britain had few roads in those days; that the only routes offering speedy transport for heavy goods were rivers and coastal seas; that on every Friday the entire population of Britain (several millions) had to eat fish; that the medieval economy was based almost entirely on exporting wool and cloth to Europe and importing

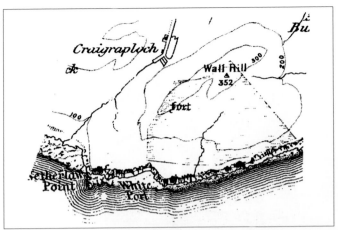

Fig.8. The tiny cove named White Port on this fragment from a Victorian map is little more than a sandy cleft in a rocky coastline. But small sailing ships carrying vital supplies for the fort on the promontory could run up the beach safely here on a rising tide.

Continental luxury goods for upper class consumption; that itinerant traders with small boats - the forerunners of men in white vans - used our coastal waters to reach beach markets large and small all around our shores.

The only requirement for a port was a flat, hard foreshore and some rudimentary protection from wind. Indeed, the existence of a flat, hard foreshore in a sheltered cove, or within the first bend of an estuary or creek, was often the sole reason for founding a settlement at that spot. Sand and shingle have a great advantage over mud and clay: they don't cling to ships' bottoms and hinder getting afloat as the tide comes in.

Wherever communities clustered together around our shores, whether in maritime cities, towns, villages, or former hamlets now reduced to a single dwelling or an isolated church or an inn or a deserted farmhouse, there was once a port that bustled with human activity. Local beaches were busy places; not used for leisure, but for commerce and industries including shipbuilding, importing/exporting of manufactured and luxury goods, repairs to fishing gear, selling of fish and landed cargoes, shore fishing and shellfish gathering, salt making and more. Flat foreshores were also important routes for people travelling without a boat. The potential for lost coins and artefacts is huge.

From a military perspective the ideal place to site an ancient or medieval fort as a defence against invasion from the sea was on a prominent cliff or hilltop that provided clear views and early warning of approaching enemy vessels. But no matter how thick its walls, every fort needed

Figs.9&10. From Roman times down to the development of weapons that rendered stone walls obsolete, a supply port was an essential part of the defences of all coastal forts. After identifying a fortress site look for ancient tracks down to a suitable cove.

Fig.10.

Fig.11. A sandy cove with a gently sloping beach, an ideal location for the growth of a port in ancient times.

supplies. Invariably they came by sea to the nearest cove that also had access routes that allowed carts and packhorses to carry food, fuel, and ammunition up to the garrison after collecting it from vessels on the foreshore.

Ports that have survived into the 21st century offer few chances to make finds from earlier ages unless extraordinary weather conditions or major civil engineering works provide opportunities to detect on material dredged from their working harbours, or to search on those rare days when harbours dry out. Better prospects await those who concentrate on coasts where modern developments have not yet swallowed up the vestiges of once busy ports, especially where the hinterland remains largely agricultural. To view an excellent example of such a coastline from the comfort of your armchair browse the Explorer OS maps covering the northern shores of the Solway Firth from the Mull of Galloway to Gretna Green. Compare your Explorers with late-19th century versions of the same maps and you will soon spot the visible remains of dozens of former ports, often at less than one-mile intervals, along the entire shoreline. If you live in that part of the country I envy your prospects. The rest of us can take heart from the fact that the foreshores and hinterlands associated with many

Fig.12. A few inshore fishing communities maintain the tradition of running up the beach to sell their catches to local people.

hundreds of former ports remain accessible in other parts of Britain. Signs to look for include: a sandy cove with a gently sloping foreshore; and low land behind the beach that may have two or more old lanes or bridleways converging on the coast. Footpaths (public and private) should lead to the same spot. If the cove is backed by cliffs, look for evidence that access to the foreshore was improved in the past (ie stone-cut steps or a cart-way cut or blasted through the cliffs to reduce the gradient so that horses could reach the beach).

Also look for local evidence of substantial medieval arable farming in the past. Don't be deterred by the sight of only one or two houses around the cove today. Walk the land up to half a mile from the cove. If you can see ridge and furrow outlines in grassed fields then ploughing once took place and a substantial medieval (or earlier) population must have lived nearby. They would certainly have established a port.

Try to locate a hamlet or small village hugging the perimeter of a cove. Its port may have prospered down to Georgian or even Victorian times. Improvements would certainly have been made during those centuries. Look for remnants of jetties, warehouses, harbour walls, cobbled and narrow lanes, old inns, reused warehouses, and docks. If the coast you have chosen is subject to silting you may encounter these structures up to half a mile inland. Any

Fig.13. Architectural clues. Dated buildings like this former inn, now a tourists' curiosity shop, hint at a once busy port.

losses in the former port will be too deep for detector searches. However, nearby arable fields will hold coins and relics lost by local people.

Search for archaeological sites nearby your area of interest. Any Roman settlement (civil or military); any Iron Age promontory fort; any medieval castle in the neighbourhood; any deserted medieval village, was located to take advantage of the sea and ships as a means of obtaining supplies. Trace access routes from these sites down to the foreshore. Jetties, quays, wharves, and warehouses might all have been built as part of the supply chain.

Fig.14. Old harbour walls. When harbour installations seem far too large for vessels using a harbour today investigate the local history. Relics from a thriving Georgian or earlier port may lie at the foot of the harbour walls and in adjacent fields.

Archaeological Finds Records

Another point of study is archaeological finds records. When 40 Bronze Age ingots of tin turned up on the foreshore of the River Erm estuary in Cornwall a few years ago the discovery was recorded as "probably part of the cargo of a Bronze Age coastal trading vessel lost in a storm three or four thousand years ago." Possibly so, but where was the port from which this ship set out? Similarly, on the Lincolnshire coast, sand more than 5ft deep was recently swept away by strong currents and high tides to reveal fish traps, saltpans and wrecks. Three weeks later all traces vanished from view when the sand was re-deposited during fresh storms. The sightings and locations were recorded, but was any attempt made to locate the settlement and port associated with the artefacts? You'll find numerous examples of your own if you browse archaeological records. Follow up your browsing with field walks and map research; take a holistic view and you may track down a lost port.

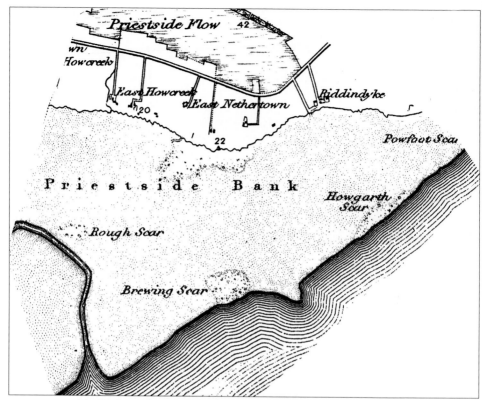

Fig.15. In northern Britain the term "scar" is often used to indicate a shingle or rocky hard on an otherwise muddy coastline. This map fragment shows four scars where vessels would have landed to off-load cargoes into horse-drawn carts or onto packhorses for trans-shipment to inland markets. Plenty of money changed hands on such spots.

Hards

Your research should also include "hards". Landing a sailing vessel on an open sandy foreshore would have presented few problems given fair wind and weather. But when mile upon mile of mud or estuarine silt and clay covered the shore, any naturally occurring outcrop of flat rock, or any geological deposit of shingle, would have taken on enormous significance as a hard spot on an otherwise soft and sticky beach. It would surely become the focus of attention for crews trying to land cargoes. A settlement would probably have sprung up on land behind the hard. Local fields - as well as the hard itself during exceptionally low tides - must hold numerous accessible losses for diligent searchers.

Fig.16. An ancient cross marking an equally ancient market site on a remote Scottish island.

Market Markers

Market markers are another point of interest in your research. On the Merionethshire coast there's a spot marked by a large standing stone and several cairns, thought to indicate an important Bronze Age port and trading centre. Ancient footpaths have been traced from the stone to the remains of abandoned copper mines several miles inland. Archaeological records show that bronze artefacts and bronze ingots have been discovered not far from the standing stone. Additionally, bronze ingots of identical composition have come to light on the Irish coast on the other side of the Irish Sea, strong evidence that Bronze Age sailors crossed and re-crossed this wide expanse of water. They would certainly have welcomed the guidance provided by the standing stone as they approached the Welsh coast. Similar standing stones indicate a market and an estuary ford on the Solway Firth, while the foreshores on which medieval pilgrims congregated (and no doubt purchased pilgrims' badges and other souvenirs) before making crossings to Whithorn, Bardsey Island and other shrines were variously marked by ancient stones and ancient trees.

We cannot know just how many markers have vanished, fallen or been swallowed by the sea. Perhaps every ancient port had a marker - a sensible arrangement for any spot located on an open beach. It might prove an interesting, hopefully profitable, exercise to seek fallen markers on coasts close to the sites of holy wells, sacred springs and monastic remains. Local folklore might also suggest places worth investigating.

Fig.17. Ancient standing stones at the confluence of two rivers flowing into a tidal estuary. This site is highly likely to have functioned as a market place in the past.

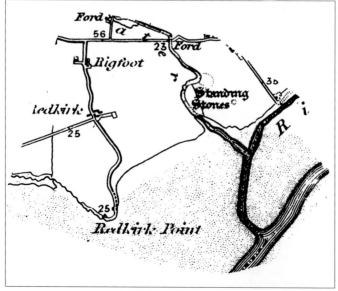

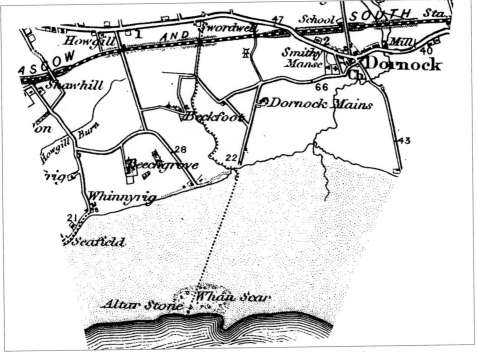

Fig.18. Another obvious candidate for an ancient market place. It's a parish boundary with a named marker stone on a hard surrounded by acres of inhospitable mud. Ancient vessels from miles around would have used this safe landing.

Fig.19. Ancient anchor.

Fig.20. Heavy hauling rings aided vessels in getting high up the foreshore.

Iron Hauling Rings

In medieval times every coastal settlement had its own fishing fleet, ranging from half a dozen to more than 100 vessels. The fleet's size depended on quantities of fish likely to be caught in the adjacent inshore waters, and on the quantities of fish likely to be sold at the fish market held on the beach once or twice each week. Successful markets caused settlements to grow; a fall in catches, or in numbers of buyers turning up at the market, sealed the settlement's fate as a declining fishing port. Silting, erosion and permanent loss of a sandy beach with enough space to haul boats above the high tide line in bad weather, were also crucial factors. Hauling the boats to safety often called for somewhere secure to attach ropes. Large anchors, some recovered from wrecks of big ships along the coast, were sometimes left on the beach for this very purpose. Alternatively one or more large iron rings were set into a rock heavy enough to withstand the worst storm. If you spot such a ring you may have located a foreshore market site where vast quantities of fish were sold over many years.

Fish Processing Facilities

By smoking and salting catches fishing families could extend their opportunities to profit from gluts of herring and mackerel. A thoroughly smoked "red herring" remains edible for weeks, and smoking could be achieved on a small scale over a simple cottage kitchen fire. But larger fleets netting enough fish to interest merchants from inland towns and cities would have had communal smokehouses and salting barrels, perhaps in a field close to the landing site. Fragmentary remains of these structures might still exist in fields not too far from the shore.

Pottery Fragments

Scatters of broken pottery often come to light on coastal foreshores. If modern they represent breakages by holiday picnickers; if Edwardian or Victorian, and in greater quantities, they may indicate coastal dumping of household refuse on a site presently suffering erosion. Earlier pottery fragments may provide clues to a former beach market and port. Coarse shards with yellow or green glaze could be pieces from large vessels used as containers for salt fish. Searches of ploughed land or allotment sites within a few yards of the coast might reveal similar fragments.

Ballast Stones

Although the beaching of small boats does not leave much in the way of archaeological remains on a foreshore, there is one tell-tale sign worth seeking: a pile of stones. They might once have formed part of an ancient fish-trap, or a busy jetty, but if the stones appear different in colour or texture to any natural rocks nearby, you may have stumbled upon a cargo of ballast stones jettisoned by a sailing vessel that came ashore to trade at a beach market. It carried a cargo of large stones to give stability under sail, and the crew had to throw the stones overboard before taking on any purchased cargo. The master of a vessel needing ballast would always use freely available stones picked up from the vessel's home beach, though there were instances of ballast stones such as flint nodules or chalk stones that could be sold when the ship beached. Nevertheless, many ballast stones ended up as abandoned piles on the foreshore.

Fig.21. The surface of a recently dug allotment in a coastal hamlet. The red pottery could be very old, or simply broken flower pots.

There's always a slim chance that a pile of stones might be from an ancient wreck driven ashore and smashed to matchwood in a violent storm. Search around all ballast stones with that hope in mind.

Farm & Field Name Evidence

As clues to a once-busy port or coastal market, any farm name or field name that draws attention to the location, or to goods sold at the market, (eg Cove Farm, or Coal Farm) merits further investigation. Names such as Drove Common and Carters' Field flanking bridleways and paths leading towards the coast may confirm that your researches are headed in the right direction.

Gaps Or Sharp Angles In Old Seawalls

In areas of deposition rather than erosion you may notice older seawalls some distance inland from the present foreshore. Gaps cut after those walls became redundant could indicate the directions of tracks used by carts and packhorses visiting the foreshore in Georgian or Victorian times. Any old seawall that takes a sudden turn in its direction must have once done so to avoid some feature no longer visible in the landscape. Detector searches in nearby fields might produce clues to a vanished site.

7. Wrecks & Hulks

At Seaton Carew, a small seaside resort in County Durham, a local man walking the coastline after a night of gales in the 1990s could scarcely believe his eyes when he spotted a substantial wooden ship lying on the foreshore where winds and currents had swept away sand. The vessel seemed intact apart from loss of ropes, rigging and some decking timbers. Who can blame him for hoping he'd stumbled on a pirate's treasure ship? In fact the craft turned out to be a late 18th century coastal trader, ballasted and probably headed for the Tyne to load coal when she got into difficulties.

A survey of wooden ship remains carried out recently on the Kentish coast around the Medway estuary recorded more than 100 hulks poking from mud, clay or sand on the shoreline. A similar walk-the-foreshore-and-count-the-wrecks exercise undertaken by enthusiasts in west Wales topped 200 discoveries, while a section of Scotland's east coast had wrecks and hulks strewn upon it at even thicker densities.

What's the explanation? Well, we must first modify our expectation that every wooden ship that ended its days on our foreshores was wrecked in a violent storm while carrying precious metals and jewellery as cargo. For hundreds, even thousands, of years small coastal trading ships laden with household goods, coal, wool or cloth bales, regularly beached to load/unload their cargoes into/from carts trundled across the sands at low tide. Even greater numbers of fishing smacks came ashore in the same way. These craft were at their most vulnerable if an unexpected storm arose while they were off-loading cargoes and catches. In that sense some were indeed wrecked, though not strictly at sea. But a more likely reason for finding the partial remains of an old wooden vessel on any foreshore is that when no longer seaworthy it was abandoned by its owner. Think of all those derelict cars dumped on roadsides in the scruffier parts of most cities and towns today. Something similar went on in centuries gone by, though the raw material - timber - offered better recycling prospects as fuel if not as spare parts.

I am as romantically attached to the dream of finding a

Fig.22. The skeletons of wooden vessels often poke above the foreshore surface when sand is washed away.

treasure wreck as the man from Seaton Carew, so let me add here that all the richly-laden wrecks still undiscovered will not be found by scuba-divers alone. The humble beachcomber and mudlark stands a chance of glory because the very coves and estuary mouths in which he/she pursues the hobby are the places where many sailing treasure ships came to grief. Their captains took them close to shore when storms broke, seeking shelter in relatively quieter waters. But the dangers were great: mud banks, sandbanks, shallow water, rocks, cliffs; if any of them combined with a wind driving hard onto the coast a sailing ship was doomed to end its days broken on the shore, perhaps spilling some of its rich cargo for 21st century beachcombers to find. This fate - driven onto a lee shore - befell numerous ships in centuries past.

There's another reason why so many remains of old wooden vessels come to light when tides and currents work in our favour. Medieval ship and boat-builders had no dry-docks or slipways. The timbers, keel, rudder and spars of the new vessel were set out during construction on a stretch of flat, sandy foreshore just above the high tide line. More often than not the new ship or boat would be replacing one that had suffered storm damage or simply

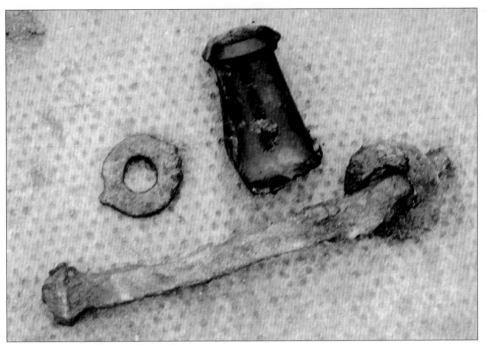

Fig.23. Medieval clench nail and two roves. I found the neck of a black glass onion bottle alongside.

become unseaworthy. Any parts from the old vessel that could be recycled in the new construction lay easiest to hand when the old craft was run aground alongside the very spot where the new work was underway. Proof of this method of working came from the discovery in the tidal Thames of new and old ships timbers screwed together, with the old providing templates for the carpenters cutting the new wood.

An average medieval coastal trader would have been about 25ft long and 9ft across its beam (=width). The method used to fix one plank to the next was termed clinker building, from an Anglo-Saxon word *clenchen*, meaning "to fix securely". It involved overlapping lengths of timber and then nailing through the overlap with iron clench nails. Each nail point passed through a washer or "rove" before the point was bent over to draw or clench the timbers tightly together. (The word "rove" comes from Viking language, an indication of the great antiquity of this building method.) If you detect near a very old foreshore hulk expect to find large numbers of iron clench nails and roves. Medieval builders tried to re-use as many nails as possible from the old ship because iron nails were very expensive. The longer the nails you find, the thicker the timbers from which they came, and the larger the ship they once held tightly together.

With no slipway to get the vessel afloat, medieval shipwrights usually waited for a high spring tide to rise sufficiently to lift the keel. Alternatively deep trenches were dug around the finished ship at low tide so that even a neap tide would rise in the trenches and float the vessel. The area where all of these activities took place would, of necessity, be a stretch of foreshore well away from places used as markets and net-mending spots on the beach. Perhaps that explains why hulks seem to come to light on rather lonely stretches of foreshore. Nevertheless, much human activity and consequent loss of possessions and artefacts must have occurred where ships and boats were built.

Towards the end of the Middle Ages a new method of shipbuilding emerged: the carvel technique in which planks were laid edge-to-edge. Now there was no need for heavy, expensive clench nails; joins could be caulked with pitch and oakum; timbers could be pre-cut to size and shape before assembly; and vessels could be much larger. The old foreshore construction methods gave way to shipbuilding in yards dug into the coastline so that work could go on irrespective of tides. But clinker-building techniques lingered on in one or two places, including the Thames estuary, where river barges were built in this style down to the 20th century.

The exposed timbers of old hulks from previous centuries are common enough on beaches and in tidal estuaries, although you will spot them only when overlying sand, shingle or mud is disturbed. Many sites have already come to light several times in the past as a result of severe weather. You'll read about some of them in local history books and archaeological reports, but you should also check local newspapers. A wreck on the shore always makes a good story, and many local newspapers have indexed their back issues. Check out the word "wreck" in the index and you will soon be making interesting discoveries down on the coastline.

Fig.24. This 18th century coastal trader was built after the age of clench nails, but it still often beached to load/unload its cargoes on hards and firm sand.

8. Sand Dunes

During the stormy winter of 1830 the sand dunes of Uig Bay on the Isle of Lewis began to erode as a result of high winds striking the shore. A local man foraging on the beach for driftwood spotted what he thought was a rabbit hole in one of the dunes. He put in his hand and pulled out the first of more than 90 pieces of ornately carved walrus tusk, afterwards identified as the stock-in-trade of a late-Viking craftsman who specialised in chess sets.

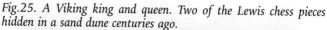

Fig.25. A Viking king and queen. Two of the Lewis chess pieces hidden in a sand dune centuries ago.

About a century earlier another storm on Lancashire's Irish Sea coast carried thousands of tons of sand several hundred yards inland. The resulting dunes totally buried the village of Ravenmoels, which has remained "lost" to this day. A similar incident in Denmark buried the village of Skagen in a single night of violent winds. Only the top of the church spire remained visible the next morning. It still protrudes from a large dune and has become something of a tourist attraction, as well as a reminder of the awesome power of nature. Back in Britain a Norfolk coastal village vanished in medieval times and its church spire, too, remained visible in the dunes. The stonework was pulled down and reused in the 1890s.

You'll see sand dunes on many British coastlines, and if you investigate local folklore you'll soon hear tales about lost coastal communities "besanded" during great storms. The fables often seem confirmed by archaeological discoveries, not all as spectacular of the Isle of Lewis chessmen, but clearly indicating that previous generations often had to abandon homes and possessions in the face of sand encroachment. Perhaps it seems strange that people chose to locate their settlements so close to unpredictable dunes, but economic history reveals that down to the early 20th century there was often more profit in managing a rabbit warren in a sand dune than in keeping dairy cows or sheep on grass.

Rabbits were big business in medieval times, with furs in as much demand as rabbit meat. Warren owners - often the local lord of the manor or the local priest - could count on two payments for every rabbit raised to adulthood. Scores of people would have earned a living from a single large warren, with management tasks including, skinning, preparing pelts for market, selling meat to butchers, fox hunting, and guarding against visits from poachers. Cheap imports of beef in the mid-19th century, together with a change of fashion that rendered skins worthless, sounded the death knell for almost all warrens. In a few places the sand combined with local soils to provide ideal growing conditions for potatoes, even asparagus, thus ensuring the survival of some communities in sand dune areas. But in

Fig.26. Free back rests and secluded spots for lovers. Expect modern as well as ancient losses when you search sand dunes.

many other places sand dunes were abandoned.

In the 20th century dunes often found a new lease of life as golf courses and nature reserves. In other areas dunes have become a source of sand, often for seaside resorts faced with erosion of their beaches by the very tides and winds that formed the local dunes.

If you have dunes on your coastline you should check archaeological records for reports of dune finds in the past, and for references to deserted coastal settlements. Any building or civil engineering developments in such areas deserve your attention. Where dunes flank popular holiday beaches they will have attracted visitors over many years. Expect modern material as well as historical discoveries in your finds bag. Nearby arable fields growing root crops should be searched thoroughly, with permission, after deep ploughing.

9. Christianity On The Coast

The acquisition of land on the coast might seem an astute move for a group of people required to eat fish throughout Lent and on every Friday of the year. However, the earliest Christians to reach Britain hugged the coastline because inshore waters offered the easiest means of transport. In early Anglo-Saxon times a coastal location for a religious settlement must have seemed a fairly safe place to monks seeking nothing more than seclusion. Early monarchs, eager to secure a place in heaven, would have felt under no earthly threat when making generous gifts of offshore islands or rocky headlands to unarmed clerics. But with ever more parcels of land donated by nobles a little further down the social scale, and with valuables pouring into the coffers during the next couple of centuries, these religious outposts became rich - prime targets for Viking raiders. By later medieval times many Christian sites had developed into shrines and places of pilgrimage for countless thousands of devotees. Difficult, often perilous journeys to distant sacred sites that offered a chance to touch a saint's bones and cure a painful disease were

Fig.27. Every religious settlement on an offshore island needed two ports to serve its lifeline for supplies from the neighbouring mainland coast. The same ports would have been used by visiting pilgrims.

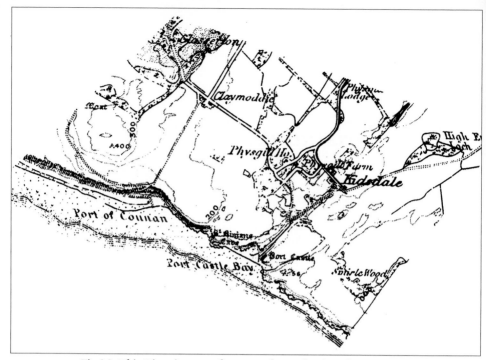

Fig.28. This Victorian map fragment shows the site of St Ninian's Cave, a famous medieval shrine. Note the two slight bays named Port of Connan and Port Castle. They hint at large numbers of pilgrims' vessels beaching here. Other coastal shrines would have had similar facilities.

undertaken every year by men and women from all walks of life. They spent a lot of money on tokens of their sacrifices - pilgrims' badges, lead ampules containing water from a holy well or spring, and medicinal compounds to apply to aching bones when they arrived safely back home.

The Church acquired yet more earthly riches when monks turned to sheep farming on a large scale in the 12th century. By this time vast tracts inland were in ecclesiastical hands and some important sites away from the coast became powerful magnets for pilgrims. At the same time many less renowned coastal shrines fell into disuse, but there were still plenty that attracted visitors and money down to the reign of Henry VIII.

How might you profit from losses associated with religious sites on the coast? Begin by studying your maps closely. Mark for further investigation (with permission won) the fields flanking all monastic remains on the coast. Also mark all isolated churches. They may have been built on the sites of early shrines. Look for places where remains of ancient Celtic crosses still stand; for wells and springs mentioned as holy places in local history books, or as having once possessed curative powers. Try to win detecting permission on any arable land close to such spots. Keep in mind the strong probability that many springs and wells will have dried up during the past 100 years. Large-scale OS maps drawn in the 1870s will have numerous springs and wells not shown on modern maps. The land around each one should be carefully searched, as should approaching footpaths.

At the same time carry out a thorough investigation of the flanking coast. Look on the old maps for clues to ancient landing places that might have been used by pilgrims. At locations where a holy place lay on an offshore island, there must have been rudimentary ports on the mainland coast and on the island in question. Trace the routes of all footpaths and bridleways that lead down to the coast. Spots where two or more old tracks crossed might have been used by medieval monks as pitches for the sale of pilgrims' badges.

Holistic thinking will alert you to the prospect of religious artefacts on associated sites. Always trace the routes of ancient tracks leading inland from religious sites on the coast. Fording places several miles from the coast may have been pitches for sales of pilgrims' badges. Churches and chapels lying on overland routes to the coast may have been places where pilgrims rested on their journeys. At cliff-top locations local history books may mention erosion of the cliffs exposing ancient coffins. Such events frequently result in grave goods ending up on adjacent foreshores.

Fig.29. An 18th century Seamen's Mission upholding a long tradition of religion on the foreshore.

10. Coastal Industries

Heavy pigs of lead stamped with Roman Imperial lettering are found on the Cheshire coast; similarly marked ingots of copper are discovered on Anglesey's foreshores; dozens of tin ingots turn up on Cornish beaches; and cakes of silver and lead have been reported from Cumbrian and Northumbrian shores. They clearly indicate not only that shipping routes were busy in ancient times, but also that exploitation of coastal resources included extraction of metal from ore veins initially exposed in cliff faces. These rich veins were mined a little further inland in later centuries, and progressively further from the coast during the next 2000 years. By medieval times the coastal metal veins were largely exhausted, but the practice of loading vessels on the beach continued with increasingly large tonnages of stone quarried from cliffs and shipped to cities and towns as building materials for cathedrals, castles, churches, town walls and more.

In the 18th and early 19th centuries slate, quarried mainly on the Welsh coast in those days, became a major industry as demand for cheap roofing materials grew. The easiest way to load a ship with heavy stone or slate is to bring the cargo alongside the vessel at the right height to lower it into the hold rather than to have to lift it over the side. This required the construction of wharves, jetties and quays on the foreshore and usually connected to the quarrying zone by a steep and narrow track that allowed mules and/or humans to haul the stone down to the waiting vessels.

Limestone occurs on or near many British coasts, especially in the north and west. It was quarried and shipped as a building material, but it had an even greater role to play in the 17th and 18th centuries in the production of fertilizer. Hundreds of limekilns - usually circular structures about ten feet in height - can be found around the coast, many at least 200 years old. In them limestone was burned with coal to produce quicklime which, after slaking, was sold to local farmers for spreading on acidic soils. Ships bringing coal to these kilns would have beached at suitable spots not far from the quarries.

Salt extraction, seaweed harvesting and the construction of tide mills on estuaries all added to coastal industrial activity in centuries past. Look out for the remains of once-busy jetties and landing stages. Finds around them in recent years have included British and foreign trading tokens, lead seals, tallies, merchants' weights and coins. Loading, unloading and selling of non-industrial cargoes would also have occurred at such sites if the landing was safe and its associated trackways led to potential customers.

Here's an excellent way to assess potential for once-busy coastal industrial sites in your county. Study a well-written book on the geology of the region.

It will tell you about commercially exploitable metal ores, minerals, building stone, chemical deposits, coal, and indeed any valuable materials that could be dug up and exported from a nearby coast. Consult 6in OS maps of areas suggested by the geological records. Cliffs will be clearly marked, as will natural and man-made access routes to the foreshore. The scale of these maps is large enough to show individual buildings, which might have been associated with a lost industry. Single-track railway lines that approach the coast might be the remains of a mineral route along which ores and other heavy materials were brought to waiting ships. Investigate accessible land around the terminal point of the line, and then work your way down to the nearby foreshore. If tidal conditions permit, and if winter storms have done their work, detect the foreshore carefully. It could be rich in lost and discarded objects associated with a time when the beach thronged to the noises of busy workers.

County museums that once devoted most of their display cases to Romano-British artefacts nowadays include 19th century relics in what they show the public. Check out the exhibits, and don't be afraid to ask members of staff if they have any examples of tallies, tokens, tools and other objects associated with long-vanished coastal industries. Try to find out (written records should be available for inspection) where these donations came from. Many museums have huge stocks of early photographs, including pictures showing coastal industries at work around the turn of the 20th century. Try to pinpoint locations on your maps. They might prove rich sources of the tallies, tokens and tools already mentioned.

11. Fresh Water

No early coastal settlement could have survived without adequate supplies of fresh water. Local springs and stream banks would have become natural focal points when women filled jugs or washed children and clothes; when sailors filled barrels; and when herdsmen drove animals to drink each day. Find an early settlement's watering places and you should find many of its artefacts. Study the oldest available OS maps on which springs and streams were clearly marked in Victorian times. The waters may have dried up or ceased to flow in modern times, but their traces, together with the ancient footpaths that converged on them, will be discernable to the careful observer. If a stream still flows onto the foreshore you are searching, trace its course inland and gain detecting permission on any arable land flanking the stream. Such a location would have made an excellent Iron Age settlement site.

12. Science & Sand

Have I stirred your interests in coastal history with what I've offered so far in this book? Are you now seriously considering a trip to a seaside location, and eagerly anticipating finds of coins and relics lost on beaches and estuarine foreshores hundreds, or even perhaps thousands of years ago? If so, I'm delighted. I want you to succeed; but not to spoil your excellent chances of success by rushing headlong into an expedition without waiting for the right weather and tidal conditions. Make no mistake: if you disregard my advice on this point you will almost certainly return from your trip empty-handed even if your historical researches guide you to a foreshore with extremely high potential for exciting finds. On the other hand, if you always work with nature, and especially if you thoroughly understand the effects of natural forces on objects lost on tidal foreshores, you will probably make finds on sites where less knowledgeable searchers return home with next to nothing.

I can think of no better use of any time you might spend at home twiddling your thumbs and waiting for nature to work on your behalf than using it to carry out a few simple experiments and observations on how objects lost on beaches are moved by the forces raging in tidal currents and storm-force winds. You can simulate currents and the effects of a storm venting its wrath on a coastal foreshore in several ways. First you'll need a handful of beach sand. Ideally this should come from the very beach on which you intend to search when conditions are right, but beach sand from anywhere will suffice. It is, of course, quite different from the sort of sand used on building sites, as you'll see if you put a spoonful in a clear glass tumbler of water and stir vigorously. Hold the glass up to the light and watch carefully as the currents created by the spoon sort the constituents of the sand by weight. Observe first that if you stir with enough vigour all the grains are initially suspended in the swirling water. Darker coloured grains, which have a lot of ferrous material in their makeup, will begin to settle first at the bottom of the glass. Lighter grains fall next, while tiny fragments of shell are the last to sink.

If you have mixer taps with a hand-held showerhead on

your bath you can carry out another interesting observation. Put the plug in the bath then pour in the remains of your sand. Run a couple of inches of water, stirring it around a little before pulling the plug. What happens next is a reversal of what happened in the glass tumbler: the lighter shell fragments shoot down the plughole at the first tug of the current; the darker grains hardly move as the water drains away. Even when you turn on the shower spray you'll have some difficulty in shifting the last of them. Stop spraying just before the dregs reach the plughole. Find a magnet and run it over the remaining grains. Most will be attracted because, as I said earlier, they consist largely of iron.

The next experiment takes us outdoors. You'll require a couple of generous handfuls of lead shot. I doubt if you'll find any these days in fishing tackle shops because the use of lead shot in angling is banned; but you should be able to obtain the small amount you need from any firm involved in the shot blasting business. If all else fails you could use small steel ball bearings bought as BB ammo for an air pistol. They don't weight as much as lead size-for-size, but they will suffice for our purposes. Next I'm going to ask you to grab a stiff broom, a hosepipe with an adjustable nozzle, a bucket and a pair of wellies. I want you to give your concrete or paved drive a thorough scrub-down. The experiment calls for a drive that abuts the side of a building, or which has concrete/stone steps at one end. If you don't have such a drive, do a good deed for any friend or family member who possesses the right type and who will appreciate watching you working at a job he/she probably hates. Don't forget to take the lead shot.

Begin by giving the drive a good dry sweeping with the stiff broom. Get rid of any grass or moss that has grown in the joints between paving slabs or between rafts of concrete, and along the line where the drive meets the flanking wall. If the drive has seen better days, scrub especially vigorously in areas where loose material has gathered in small potholes caused by weathering. Once all the dry brushing is completed sprinkle the lead shot fairly evenly across the surface of the drive.

Now for the water. Adjust the nozzle so that the hose gives a wide and fairly gentle spray. Squat low to the ground and fan the water across the drive in the direction of the flanking wall. Miniature waves will wash across the drive as your arm gets into a steady rhythm. You'll see at once that you have created the effects of a tide running up a beach on a calm day towards what we can now call a sea wall. Keep the gentle spray going at the same angle and force for about five minutes, then turn off the water and hunt for those hundreds of lead shot you put down earlier. The majority should now be trapped in the joints you cleaned out before you began hosing, or in depressions from which you cleared loose material when sweeping; but quite a few will have been carried all the way to the wall. If there's a gap at that point the lead shot will have fallen into it.

Now for a simulated storm. Increase the power of the spray; give it four times the force, but remain in your squatting position and spray the water in the same pattern you used earlier. Let it wash across the drive for five minutes, then check on the lead shot. Little, if any, will have moved from the joints, cracks, crevices and depressions it fell into when you applied the gentler spay.

Now let's simulate a storm that reaches the peak of its frenzy at a period when a rising spring tide strikes a sea-wall. Stand up and spray the water along the base of the wall so that its full force hits the gap where lead shot is lodged. Spray at maximum force for about a minute, then turn off the tap and inspect the base of the wall. Some of the lead shot will have been displaced; but I expect you to be surprised by the numbers of lead shot that have resisted the full force of the water and remained in the gap.

Now we'll simulate a storm that reaches full fury at a period when a neap tide rises only to a midway point on the beach. From your standing position direct the hose so that water splashes across the middle of the drive. After one minute at maximum pressure inspect that area. I'm sure you will observe that this time many of the trapped lead shot have been dislodged from their gaps, cracks, and crevices. They may be lying fully exposed on the flat areas of the drive. Revert to the gentle spraying with which you began and those exposed balls of lead will quickly disappear into the nearest holes.

Make one final observation before we leave the drive. Allow water still on the surface to soak away or to evaporate if you chose a warm day. Watch the surface of the drive and note that some spots drain or dry out quicker than others. Areas around cracks, fissures and depressions hold water and stay wetter for longer.

What does all that messing about with sand grains, a few gallons of water, a handful of lead shot and a magnet tell us about real conditions down at the coast? Well, we should learn from the experiments that sand on any beach shifts when a tide sweeps over it. How much depends on strength of tides and currents: during relatively calm weather the top two or three inches of sand transform to a state of flux as the tide flows up the beach; during stormy weather the beach to a depth of 2ft or 3ft can be picked up and carried as easily as those few grains were swirled in your glass tumbler.

The drive you scrubbed represents the firm foundation upon which most beaches rest. And like your drive, this underlying stratum has cracks, gaping holes and worn depressions across its surface. Heavy objects - lead fishing weights, gold sovereigns, lost jewellery, copper, silver and brass artefacts - will behave in precisely the same way as your experimental lead shot. They will move when tides and currents have enough strength to carry them, and they will find their way into the cracks and depressions where they will sit until an even stronger tide, current or crashing wave winkles them out.

The hose squirting at full force against the back wall of the drive represents a spectacle we all associate with stormy weather at the coast when giant waves strike a resort's seawall and send showers of spray and salt water crashing onto the promenade. Many detectorists, including some who spend a lot of time on coastal sites, imagine that working a popular beach after such a storm is bound to produce numerous finds. I agree that a lot of discoveries will occur after the top end of the beach has taken a battering from a high spring tide; but I also have to point out that

Fig.30. I Hope this sepia postcard from 1930s Bognor reproduces well enough for inclusion here because its two lower photographs show very clearly the different effects of wave action during a spring tide storm and a neap tide storm. In the photograph at lower right the sea wall takes a severe pounding. Some sovereigns lost by Victorian visitors who sat close to the wall would probably be disturbed by these mighty waves; but any gold coins trapped in crevices at the bottom of the wall would not budge. In the photograph at lower left the breakers are churning sand and shingle at a midway point on the beach, their power is probably reaching the very foundation layer when the neap tide goes out it will leave sovereigns on or very close to the surface.

much of the storm's energy was dissipated, even wasted, on battering the immovable seawall with powerful waves. The sand immediately in front of the wall will receive a thorough "ploughing" from breakers, bringing losses in this area to the surface or very close to the surface. But any losses that found their way into cracks and crevices hard up against the wall may escape disturbance altogether. Far better, in my opinion, to work on a beach or foreshore that has no seawall to protect it when a powerful storm combines with a high spring tide.

When you sprayed the middle of the drive at full force you simulated a neap tide combining with a storm. (Neap tides result from the gravitational influences of the moon and sun working against each other, rather than together as when a spring tide occurs. A neap tide can be expected about a fortnight after a spring tide.) In nature this coupling often proves quite devastating for sandy beaches. With no seawall to take the brunt, breakers will crash onto unprotected sand and probably sweep it away to a depth of several feet - often down to the very foundation on which the beach rests. Bonanza conditions await any detectorists who plan their trips to coincide with these conditions.

A thick covering of sand had to be left to your imagination when you worked on the drive. The cracks, fissures, depressions all lay fully exposed from the outset. How, you might wonder, can similar features be identified on a beach where the sand is anything but imaginary? Fortunately there are two or three ways in which you can locate the places where non-ferrous objects might have come to rest, even on beaches where blankets of sand cover losses from the past. You will recall that I brought to your notice the fact that the concrete drive dried out in a patchy manner following its hosing, and that the places remaining wettest for longest all lay close to cracks, fissures and depressions. The same applies on most beaches. Spend a couple of hours watching the tide retreat after high water. You will soon spot areas where seawater lingers longer. You might even notice pools on the beach, clear indications of depressions in those wet areas. Mark each of these spots on your map for future reference. On a day when you arrive at

Fig.31&32. Clear evidence of gullies and depressions in the foreshore is shown in these two seaside postcard views. The ragged nature of the falling tide lines confirms an uneven beach. Detecting where the wet fingers of salt water remain should produce finds when a neap storm ploughs the sand at those spots.

the beach at low tide, observe the tide line as the sea begins to creep back up the beach. If it makes sudden rushes at one or two places, sending out fingers of seawater ahead of the main line, you have further evidence of fissures beneath the surface. Mark them for future reference.

If a stream crosses your chosen beach it provides visible evidence of a geological fissure because the fresh water running off the land has used the crack in the beach's foundation as its bed. The stream may peter out when it approaches the low water mark, but if you dig a trench at that spot you will find the fissure. Stormy weather and a neap tide might dislodge losses trapped in it. Mark the area on your map for future reference.

Places where the sand remains wet as the tide falls probably overlie depressions in the beach's foundation. Dig a few trial trenches to a depth of one or two feet, examining the sand grains as you dig. Do the sand grains become coarser or darker? Can you see black sand or any fragments of man-made metal? If lugworms have been at work in the area their casts bring up sand from as much as one foot below the surface. Examine the casts. If they contain black sand, you have no need to dig further. Mark the area on your map for future reference.

Broad expanses of sand devoid of clues such as uneven tide lines, wet patches, pools, streams or black sand, can be dismissed as potentially unproductive provided you have no written evidence about finds made when mud or clay was exposed at moments when the beach lost its sand during heavy storms. If finds have been made in the past, dig a trial trench to ascertain the present depth of sand overlying the mud or clay. A covering only one or two feet deep will be highly susceptible to movement during a heavy storm combined with a neap tide. Mark the area on your map for future reference.

Let me assume that you have completed all of your historical research and map marking, and that you have heeded the advice to wait for the right weather conditions: a spring tide and a coastal storm if your beach has no backing wall; a neap tide and a coastal storm if you have identified plenty of potential bonanza gullies in the middle

Figs.33&34. When a high spring tide strikes a solid sea wall it makes plenty of splashes but does little damage. When the waves strike an unprotected coast they tear into the land, wash away loose soil and other small particles, leaving stones, pottery fragments, perhaps metal artefacts exposed on the foreshore for several days. Get there at the right time to reap the rewards.

Fig.34.

areas of your beach. Tide tables giving high and low water predictions for months ahead at all coastal ports can be viewed on the Internet. You can also obtain coastal weather forecasts from the same source. They seem fairly reliable for up to a week ahead, so you have no excuse for not being on the spot when the forces of nature strike in your favour.

Suitably clad against the elements, and equipped with the right type of detector, you can begin to work the beach as soon as the tide turns. Early indications that massive sand movement has occurred will be piles of loose sand and/or shingle where none existed on your previous trip.

Work the gullies and the beach around them as soon as you can get at the spots where records indicate likely losses in the past. If areas of mud, clay or peat have become exposed, many losses will lie on the surface, held by the sticky matrix and often visible to the naked eye. Grab them while you can. On some foreshores where underlying mud or clay occurs you may encounter large pebbles, even boulders, stuck fast in the foundation material. If you make finds in the mud or clay alongside it's worth manhandling some of the boulders and casting them aside so that you can search beneath them. They often trap losses - especially heavy gold and lead.

Violent storms make good headlines. The local newspaper circulating in the locality that has attracted your attention will have records of numerous storms during the past century. Find out if the paper has been indexed and if copies of the index are held at the local library. If not you could contact the newspaper's librarian directly and try to win permission to read cuttings about storms in the past. The usefulness of reports from years gone by lies in what they say about what happened to beach sand when storms hit the coast. Cross-referencing with tidal records from previous years will tell you what to expect when spring and neap tides coincide with stormy weather. If luck is on your side you may discover newspaper photographs showing peat beds, wrecks, former landing stages, fossils and more. If you can identify the spots you'll have a head start when the next storm hits the coast.

Fig.35. The depth of sand on a beach alters dramatically during storms. Look out for mounds of the stuff against beach huts if you get to the coast after a storm and you want to judge the effects of the recent weather. Council workmen will bulldoze the sand back to a deep and level covering across the entire foreshore before summer visitors arrive.

13. 5,000 Years On A Foreshore

One of the fascinations of searching along a few hundred yards of shoreline lies in surprise finds. They can range from ancient flint implements to Edwardian sovereigns. Here I want to throw some light on how it came about that man-made artefacts separated in time by thousands of years could eventually lie in such close proximity on a stretch of beach. Let's begin by imagining what a modern beach might have looked like 50 centuries ago. The place I'm trying to picture has/had features that will occur on most beaches; I've put them together here as a generalized example. My imagined beach lies on what is now Britain's eastern edge, where much of the present-day coastline would have been grassland dotted with open woods in 3,000 BC, a place where people came to graze their animals and to collect flint nodules from which to make their exquisite arrowheads and cutting blades. During the next 2,000 years humans developed metalworking skills. With their new tools they began to cut down the woodlands and to convert some of the grassland to arable. In their busy lives they must have experienced the loss of many of their possessions in the soil. Those artefacts mingled with earlier losses of flint tools and weapons that had belonged to previous generations.

Around 1,000 BC human lives were dramatically affected by the sea: it began to creep inland, turning arable and pasture into salt marsh. Humans responded by altering their diet and their way of life. Shellfish, especially oysters, became an important source of nourishment; seabirds and their eggs were sought in the marshes, where many arrows and spears became lost in the heat of the chase. Domestic animals were driven down to the wetlands to fatten on lush grasses and reeds. Women did a lot of the herding so losses of personal adornments such as brooches inevitably occurred. Fishing from small boats, as well as the construction of fish traps, now occupied much of the lives of the entire community. Further losses of men's possessions and tools joined those dropped on what had once been dry land.

By AD 500 the sea had swallowed the marshes and a sand beach had begun to form where cattle once grazed. Now the humans had the tools and equipment to counterattack. They built sea defences including walls to hold back the tides. They constructed a small breakwater to protect fishing boats and to defend the sandy foreshore so that larger trading ships could sail up the beach, taking advantage of the hard and establishing a market. The locals also built low walls to trap the sea and evaporate it to make salt to sell at the market alongside fish and other produce.

By 1300 the sea had overwhelmed the defensive walls, burying the ancient breakwater and one or two old boats under several feet of sand. More local farmland on the coastal margin was lost, but the extended beach still attracted trading ships; the fishing fleet had also increased and new farmland was won from surrounding forests and protected by a stouter seawall. Sheep grazing the new pastures brought economic benefits. There was more money for everybody, and more coins to lose while working on the beach. Prosperity seemed assured - until the Black Death wiped out more than half the local workforce.

By 1700 the settlement had shrunk to a fishing village. It lost prominence as a trading centre when bigger ports further along the coast took advantage of their estuary locations where large ships could dock at all stages of the tide. Small fishing boats designed for local conditions meant that the community could still feed itself and sell surplus dried fish to merchants who came to the village with packhorse teams. Farming suffered economic depression, but the bounty of the sea seemed never-ending. The local beach remained a busy working area.

By 1900 the yearly shoals of herring and cod had failed to come to inshore waters for several seasons. Some families left the village when husbands signed on as crew aboard ocean-going trawlers. Only half a dozen boats continued with inshore fishing. Then came the railway, and a rich entrepreneur who built a promenade, a pier and a grand hotel. Tourists with gold sovereigns now enjoyed the golden sands, losing their own gold and knowing nothing of the ancient and medieval losses that lay beneath their feet. In winter months, when nature exposed the secrets during brief storms and lashing tides, the tourists were never around to discover them.

14. Groynes

No book dealing with our coastline can neglect a class of structures which, taken together, probably amount to man's greatest effort to alter, or at least control, natural occurrences on the 6,000 miles of foreshore that surround us. I refer to groynes, a word of some antiquity, meaning, in Vulgar Latin, a pig's snout. In the 1600s it was first applied to squat timber constructions jutting out from the top of a beach and thrusting, just like a pig's snout, towards the sea. Their purpose: to combat the effects of a phenomenon known as longshore drift, which gradually and inexorably pushes sand in a clockwise direction (with a few exceptions) around the British Isles.

Coastal holiday resorts were unknown in those days; the sand's importance lay in the protection it gave to arable and pasture acres flanking the shore, and its even greater importance in providing relatively easy places for boats and small ships to beach for reasons already discussed. The cost in man-hours and materials must have been substantial, and everyone in a coastal community had to contribute towards groyne building with either money or labour. Nor was it a one-off charge: timber groynes suffered regular damage from pounding waves, making replacement or extensive repairs urgent necessities. In 200 or more years of timber groynes the entire system must have been renewed scores of times.

Iron groynes did not make an appearance until the late 19th century, followed by even uglier concrete after the Second World War. I'm delighted to see that the very latest fashion in groynes involves dumping huge boulders, each half the size of a family car, in vertical piles running down the beach and sometimes along it. I hope these prove successful because they seem ideal places for colonies of crabs to take up residence and I can think of nothing tastier that an edible crab caught in a rock crevice and boiled over a driftwood fire!

Victorian 6in OS maps recorded accurately the positions of thousands of timber groynes around our coasts. The metal and concrete types that replaced them were usually built a few yards from the damaged timber ones, partly because it saved the trouble of digging out any remaining

Fig.36. Man's efforts to halt or at least to slow down longshore drift, the gradual clockwise movement of sand and shingle around our coasts, has resulted in ten of thousands of groynes sprouting from beaches. They come in all shapes and sizes, and they all act as traps for losses ancient and modern. (Gaps in the groynes shown here provide access for fishing boats and other small craft.)

Fig.37. Groynes have always provided backrests, windbreaks and focal points for visitors. Whether organising a beach picnic or posing for a family photograph, you'll find no better patch of beach than that alongside a groyne to claim as your own during a summer holiday. But as a winter treasure hunter detect around the groyne months after visitors have departed and a neap tide storm has swept away a lot of the sand and shingle. You'll soon discover that an old groyne can make a very profitable site.

foundations; but also because the engineers appreciated that even a small amount of timber left beneath the surface would continue to assist in holding sand on the beach. With the aid of the appropriate Victorian OS map, and careful observation as a high tide falls, many vanished groyne sites can be discovered by the tell-tale wetness mentioned in the section of this book headed "Science & Sand". A trench dug on such a spot can produce excellent results in Victorian losses. It's also an ideal place to use sieving methods on days when no storms are predicted and the only way to reach buried finds is to dig for them.

Fig.38. My wooden framed sieve has a plastic mesh so that I can use it in combination with a detector. It has given several seasons of good service, but it's rather heavy for lugging across broad beaches. If you design your own sieve follow the suggestions in the text on how to make a lightweight version.

The homemade sieve in my treasure hunting kit is a robust piece of equipment made from half-inch timber boards and quarter-inch heavy-duty plastic mesh. It's far too heavy to carry on my long cycling trips to potential sites and I only use it on tidal foreshores very close to home. But I recently saw a father and son team at work with a much lighter sieve around an old timber groyne on a Kent foreshore. It was a very simple sieve made from a plastic bread tray that had come from a baker's van. A hole roughly 1ft square had been cut in the tray, and the gap then covered with rigid plastic mesh (quarter-inch) bought at a DIY superstore. The whole device was light enough for the lad, aged about twelve, to carry across the beach. His dad could fill it with two or three shovelfuls of sand from the trench. The lad then swept a detector head across it, and the father threw the contents as backfill into one end of the trench. The boy had plenty of positive non-ferrous signals to investigate, some from losses trapped alongside the old groyne for more than a century. I'm planning to copy the design as soon as I can find an unwanted bread tray.

Fig.39. These remains of wooden groynes show clearly that the old structures will obviously act as traps for beach losses so long as tides and currents never gain the strength to wash away the timbers. Note the pooling of water at the seaward ends, a sign of man-made gullies around the foundations where large boulders hold fast to the stoutest members.

15. Sovereigns On The Foreshore

I have already discussed experimenting with lead shot. I wish it was possible to do something similar with gold shot (if gold can be bought in that form) but I don't want to take responsibility for numerous readers losing the noble metal in cracks and crevices on their drives. Please take my word for it when I tell you that your hosepipe would need to work at twice the pressure in order to push gold around in the way it moved lead. And a tiny gold ball trapped in a gap along the back wall would resist your efforts to dislodge it until you turned the tap full on. Yes, gold can prove exceedingly stubborn, especially gold in the almost pure 22ct form it came in when sovereigns and half-sovereigns were legal tender in every shop in the land.

Production of these famous coins, with their magnificent depiction of St George and the Dragon on the larger of the two, commenced in 1817 and continued with occasional changes in design, but always with the same purity of gold and accurate weight of coin (8gr for the sovereign; 4gr for the half) down to 1914. Millions went into circulation during those 97 years - more than all other British gold coins minted before 1817 put together - and tens of thousands disappeared from circulation to the puzzlement and disappointment of the men at the Mint. This massive

Fig.40. These are what we are after: miniature works of art in almost pure gold. Tens of thousands lie on beaches around Britain. They are deeply buried and you will need all the skills and knowledge gained by reading this book to win your share from the foreshore.

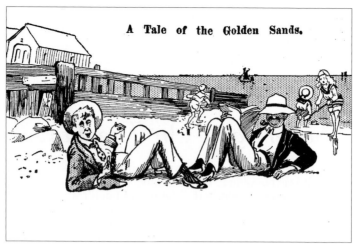

A Tale of the Golden Sands.

1.–Tompson (who has been lazily ro'lling on the sands):
"HULLO, TOODLES, HERE'S A SOVEREIGN, I DECLARE!" (JOY).

2.–"WELL, I'M BOTHERED! HERE'S ANOTHER ONE IN
ALMOST THE SAME SPOT!" (MORE JOY).

Fig.41. Regular readers of Treasure Hunting magazine may recognize this cartoon strip. I used it in 1992 as an illustration for a feature titled "Detecting & Collecting The 20th Century". It merits reprinting here not only because it's about sovereigns lost on a public beach, but also because it shows that even as late as the Edwardian era young men still walked abroad with several pounds in gold slipped casually in trouser pockets. And where are the young men sprawled on the sand and losing their sovereigns? Why, right alongside a wooden groyne!

3.–"And yet another! Why, it's a perfect gold mine" (still more joy).

4.–"Well, there don't seem to be any more, so here's half-a-crown for you youngsters to celebrate my good fortune."

5.–(Later) "Eh? What? Dropped it out of my pocket while I was sprawling on the sand? My own money? Well! So it is!"

increase in personal and very portable wealth coincided with Britain's rise to economic dominance in the world. Of course, there was still poverty of Dickensian proportions throughout our nation; nevertheless more people were relatively better off than at any time in British history. Increasing wealth led gradually to increased leisure time. And no form of leisure attracted greater crowds than that of sea bathing.

It began as a medicinal cure for gout and skin ailments suffered by members of the aristocracy, with seawater spa baths patronized by the monarch and his courtiers. The upper middle classes followed suit during the next few decades, taking to the sea at Brighton, Scarborough, Weston-super-Mare, Margate, Hastings, Folkestone and one or two other locations from which the aristocracy departed as those further down the social ladder made their appearance.

Visitor numbers at Brighton rose from 7,000 in 1818 to 20,000 in 1840, swiftly followed by thronging crowds at other resorts who benefited from the newfangled steam train network, which soon began to challenge coastal shipping companies for tourist business.

In class-conscious Victorian society, segregation went far beyond the first, second and third-class railway carriages that, by the mid-1800s, carried most visitors to the coast. At many resorts lower middle class visitors, such as post office clerks and junior managers in department stores, were actively discouraged by council regulations that refused or blocked applications for licences to open relatively inexpensive boarding houses. Prices at main seafront hotels were kept prohibitively high and bookings for short stays refused. Day-trippers, the Victorian seaside resort equivalent of today's *Big Issue* vendors, were doubly deterred by practices such as locating charabanc terminals miles from the seafront, or by ensuring that cheap excursion trains arrived at secondary rather than main stations. Even today we hear of seaside resorts that seek to ban amusement arcades, ice-cream vendors and metal detectorists, with most of the gate keeping enforced by those who value exclusivity over democracy.

Fig.42. Site clues on a postcard. The floral gardens and ornate pier confirm the status of an upper class Victorian resort (Eastbourne). Despite the high tide, the tops of groynes protecting the beach can just be seen above high water mark. They would be excellent spots on which to concentrate a search after both spring and neap tides as there is little in the way of sea wall at the top of the beach.

The social history of the British seaside from the middle of Victoria's reign to the outbreak of the First World War is a story of rearguard actions by middle class families and ferocious assaults on social barriers by the working classes. The middles resolved to patronize resorts where strolls along quiet promenades, picnics in ornate gardens, maidenly pursuits such as collecting pebbles, fossils and seashells, afternoon teas in hotel foyers and discreet dips in the sea from the steps of bathing machines drawn up on sexually segregated beaches were the highlights of month-long holidays in July and August.

Working-class families, freed from factory drudgery for one day a week, and with two or three bob in spending money burning a hole in their pockets, hankered after fun fairs, whelk stalls, donkey rides, ice-cream and pots of tea bought from a stall on the beach. In the long run the working masses won, but by that time nobody carried gold sovereigns in pockets and purses.

How can you improve your chances of finding sovereigns and half-sovereigns at the coast? Here are the golden rules:

1. Study local newspaper archives in coastal towns that once attracted middle class Victorians and Edwardians. You'll find lots of advertisements for bathing machines and other foreshore attractions. Mark your OS maps with the precise locations of these facilities, together with spots where deckchairs were erected on the beach. Articles in the newspaper will probably cover events such as the opening of pleasure gardens and promenades, or give advice to visitors about walks and carriage drives to local beauty spots, view points and picnic sites. Mark all of them on your maps for further investigation with detectors suited to those types of sites.

2. Winter editions of the local newspaper will carry reports of major storms, together with useful information about what the Borough Engineer did to combat storm damage and protect those all-important sands against longshore drift. Careful measurements taken from Victorian 6in maps should enable you to pinpoint 19th century groynes. Mark them carefully as sites to investigate when storms strike, or when you visit the beach during calmer weather and want to try your hand at digging and sieving for sovereigns.

3. Form a collection of Victorian/Edwardian postcards from the resort of your choice. Photographs packed with clues to good sites can be found in old albums. Seek them in local junk shops.

4. Look for architectural clues when investigating minor towns and villages that may have prospered as resorts for only a few years. Hotel frontages that now seem much too grand; forsaken band-stands; the remnants of piers and ostentatious promenades, all give clues to where people with gold in their pockets once gathered in numbers.

5. Have sufficient patience to await the right weather and tidal conditions.

6. Never forget that gold losses on any site will lie deeper than all other losses. Make sure your detector can perform at the right depths and be sure to dig deep enough when trying your hand at non-detecting methods.

7. Try to obtain information (perhaps from local detectorists or beachcombers) about where any sovereigns and half-sovereigns have been found on the foreshore in the past. Because of their uniformity of weight and shape other sovereign losses will turn up again on the same spots.

Fig.43. Southwold's latest pier (opened 2001) is the first to be built in Britain for 50 years. It's predecessor (opened 1900) brought middle class visitors to Southwold aboard steamers that docked at the pier's end. Much of the wooden structure was swept away during a storm in 1934, but by that time lots of sovereigns had been lost beneath and around the pier. They make Southwold a place worth visiting at the height of the next big storm.

GREAT BOOKS FROM GREENLIGHT

 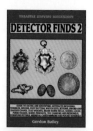  

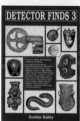   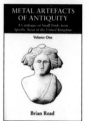

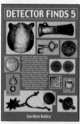   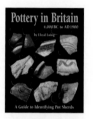

  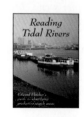 

Greenlight Publishing, 119 Newland Street, Witham, Essex CM8 1WF
Tel: 01376 521900 Fax: 01376 521901
email: books@greenlightpublishing.co.uk www.greenlightpublishing.co.uk